SOCIAL WELFARE DEPARTMENT N.G.Os & THEIR WORKING

AFSHAN QURESHI

The SOCIAL WELFARE DEPARTMENT, NGOs &THEIR WORKING

Afshan Qureshi
Scholar of Sociology
Bahauddin Zakaria Uuiversity
Multan

The welfare of the people in particular has always been the alibi of tyrants.
Albert Camus.
Power has only one duty - to secure the social welfare of the People.
Benjamin Disraeli.

Contents

Introduction

All District are controlled by DCO (District Coordination Officer), no one or any political party cannot enter in any district without his permission. Here we see the scenario of Multan District. Here is also a DCO who controlled all the departments of District Multan. In his under, there is present 6 EDO (Executive District Officer) in different 6 departments Health, Education, Finance, Community Development, Municipal Services & Law. In this chapter, our focus is on Community Development. EDO has controlled all departments which are related from his field. Under the Edo (CD), there is working 7 DO (District Officer) in Cooperative, Labor, Special Education, Social Welfare, Sports, Culture & CO. But in this assignment, our main focus is on Social Welfare Department.

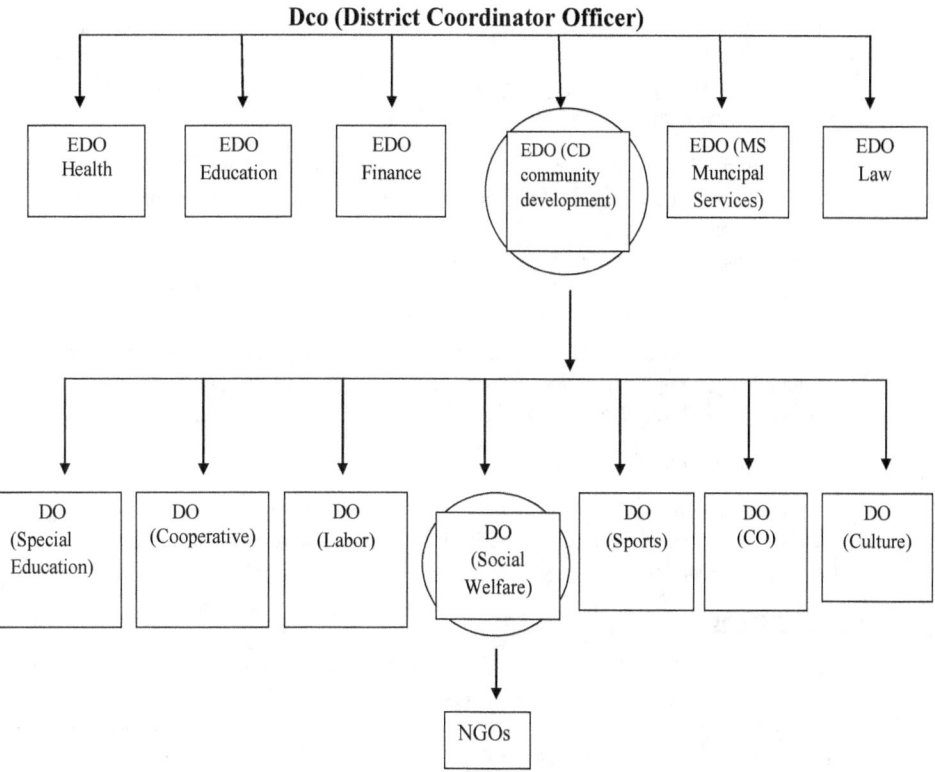

Community Development & It's Basic Departments

Community Development

Community Development is a process by which

- The efforts of people are united with the government authorities
- To improve the economic, social & cultural conditions of communities
- To integrate these communities into the life of nation
- To enable them
- To contribute fully
- To national progress

Special Education Department

To educate the physically & mentally handicapped children in an ordinary schools or classrooms which they cannot get in the common class rooms. The only aim is to give education to special children that to make them enable that they live a better life with respect & dignity. There are some special education schools names of Multan.

- Govt. Special Education Centre, Jalapur Pirwala, Near Civil Hospital, Multan
- Govt. Special Education Centre, Shujaabad House # 7 W Block, New housing Colony Lodhran Road. Multan
- Govt.Special Education Centre, Bosan Town.Multan
- Umeedgah Centre for Special Children Gulzeb Colony # 2, Street # 32 Vehari Road, Multan
- Kaus-e-Kaza 3 Bosan Road Nasheman Colony Chungi 6 Opp. Hamza Masjid, Multan
- Govt. Shadab Training Institute for Special Education, X Block satellite Town, DEO Office Madni Chowk, New Multan

Cooperative Department

It is a sometime of farm, business, or other organization which is owned and run jointly by its members, who share the profits or benefits. In Multan, it is working on the projects of societies such as Wapda town etc.

Labor Department

The Department of Labor works to promote the welfare of the job seekers, workers, labors & retirees. The aim of this department is to improve the working conditions and create opportunities for their employment. It also works to protect retirement and healthcare benefits, help employers to find workers, strengthen collective bargaining, and track changes in employment, prices and other national economic measurements. The Department also administers a variety of the laws of labors. Eg: shops, hotels, factories, mills etc.

Sports Department

All the activities of sports are held in district. To manage & spread the news to people about sports that mostly people take participation & do enjoy with some rules & regulations.

Culture Department

All Seminars, drama programs, singing & poetry consults are held by this department by with some rules & regulations for the enjoyment of people, eg In Multan Art Council, Punjab Youth Festivals etc.

CO Department

This department is controlled all the system of union councils, to manage all bio data of population, to take all records of birth, death, migration of people of this UC. In Multan, there is working 129 Union Councils.

Social Welfare Department

Social welfare department should have the skills, the feelings of humanity & also to be professional. They have to work for the well being of society & try to solve all the problems which are related to social welfare of society.

Social Welfare Department

Social Welfare Department:

The organized public or private social services are for the assistance of disadvantaged groups. Social welfare department should have the skills, to be professional & the feelings of humanity. They have to work for the well being of society & try to solve all the problems which are related to social welfare of society.

Functions of Social Welfare Department:

There are some important functions of Social Welfare Department which are as followed.

- To determine the purpose, aims & objectives of the organization.
- To establish the structure of the organization & keeping the organization strong
- Directing the work of organization, selecting & developing an able & adequate staff.
- Working with boards & committees.
- Looking ahead forecasting.
- Providing financial administration.
- Maintaining effective public relations
- To maintain proper coordinate with other agencies

Units of Social Welfare Department:

There are some units of Social Welfare Department which are as followed.

1. Social Welfare Complex MDA Chowk , Multan
2. Mother & Children Home (Dara ul Falah)
3. Dara ul Aman
4. Blood Transfusion Unit, Nishter Hospital Multan
5. Model Drug Abuse Centre, Nishter Hospital Multan
6. Urban Community Development Project No. 1. MDA Road , Multan
7. Urban Community Development Project No. 2. MDA Road , Multan
8. District Industrial Home (Sanutzar), MDA Road , Multan
9. Aaffiuat, Near Jamia Mehria, Shumsabad Colony Multan
10. Convalescent Home (Rahat), Near Dehar Chowk, Matti Tul Road Multan
11. Hostel for Working Women, MDA Road Multan
12. Government Nigheban Centre, Behind Health Department: Complex, Kutcheri Road Multan.
13. SSP Medicine, Nishter Hospital Multan
14. Gehwar, Near Dehar Chowk, Matti Tul Road Multan
15. Drug Rehabilitation Centre
16. Panah

17. Chairman District Bait-ul-mal Committee
18. Women Welfare Department (now it is abundant from social welfare, make its own department)
19. Social Welfare Department, Children Hospital Complex Multan
20. SOS Village

What is Social Work?

According to W.A. Fried Lander, "Social Work is a professional service based upon the scientific knowledge & skills in human relations that assists individual or groups to obtain the social & personal satisfaction & independency"

If a blind person stand on the road & one person come there, & ask him what are you doing, where he want to go & hold his hand & help him to cross the road or send to his destination. It is called social work. In as like social works there have not any personal benefit it is totally based on humanity.

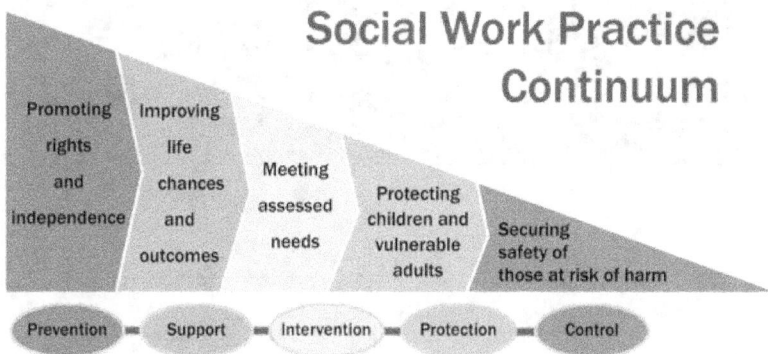

Social work is an enabling profession in which we use the solving process to resolve the problems of society such as women rights, women violence, unemployment, poverty, illiteracy, child labor, drug abuse, environment pollution etc.

Principles of Social Work

Basic principles of social work are as followed.

- Acceptance
- Good Communication
- Capacity of Accepting every problem of every community
- Understanding of felt needs & resources
- Participation

- Confidence
- Self knowledge
- Self discipline
- Humanity Feelings
- Good ethics
- Liberator
- Meaningful relationship with people
- Progressive program experience
- Resource Mobilization
- Evaluation

Types of social work

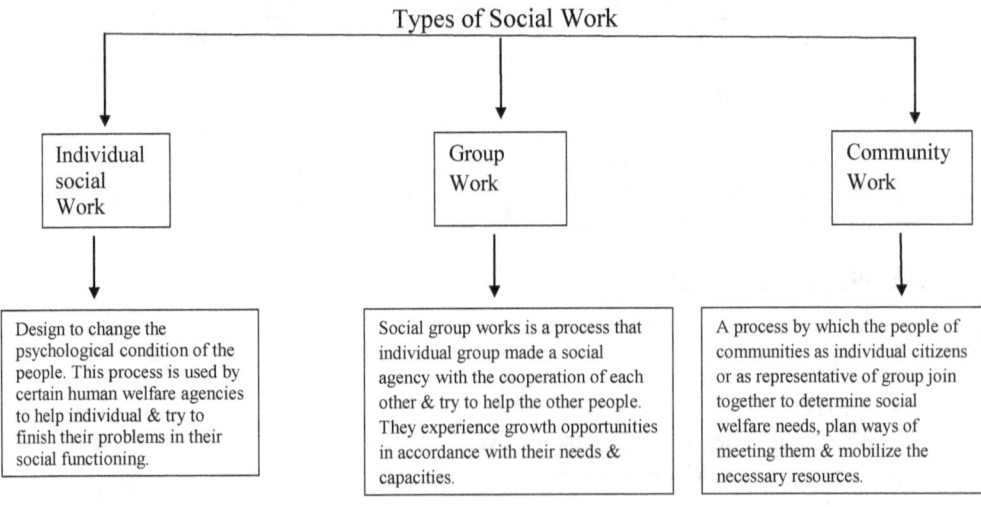

Types of Social Work

Individual social Work

Design to change the psychological condition of the people. This process is used by certain human welfare agencies to help individual & try to finish their problems in their social functioning.

Group Work

Social group works is a process that individual group made a social agency with the cooperation of each other & try to help the other people. They experience growth opportunities in accordance with their needs & capacities.

Community Work

A process by which the people of communities as individual citizens or as representative of group join together to determine social welfare needs, plan ways of meeting them & mobilize the necessary resources.

Non Government Organization

What is NGO?

NGO stand for Non Governmental Organization. More than 1 Lack NGOs are working in Pakistan. They are working for the welfare of society. In 1945, we know the concept of NGOs. They are totally independent from government control. They don't see the challenges of government. They are totally based on non-criminal. They do not involve in any political party. There are mostly organizations are NPOs (Non Profiting Organization). Mostly Issues of NGOs are illiteracy, poverty, human rights, women, student & child welfare etc.

MOU (Memorandum of Understanding)

MOU (Memorandum of Understanding) is a legal document or argument between government & NGOs. It is based upon the requirements & responsibilities of both government & NGOs.

No anyone international NGO cannot give direct fund to Local NGOs. When International NGO completes the process of the agreement of MOU then they can give the fund to local NGO & take their works with them. After the agreement of MOU with government, International NGO also do the agreement with the local NGOs.

NOC (Non Objection Certificate)

After signing of MOU, NGOs have to sign the agreement of NOC with provisional level. After this they have the authority to do their work without any conflict or fear.

Registration Process of NGOs:

- Name of NGO
- Address
- Office Furniture
- Staff
- Present Services
- Future Program
- Preparation of Record
- Bank Account Number
- Sources of Income
- Conference Proceeding Meeting
- Membership Register (22 members are necessary at division & district level but at provisional level, 500 members are necessary)
- Dairy & Dispatch Register
- Visit Book

- Membership Forum
- Voucher Book of Department
- 3 Affidavit

(Those people who registered their NGOs it is necessary for them that their relation is not with any political or religious party. They have paid 100 rupees according to the article fee in the account of 1441 in Punjab Bank. Those NGOs are based on district level they have to pay 2500)

Registration Acts of NGOs:

There are some contents articles of Registration Process of NGOs. These acts are as followed.

- Article 1. Name of Agency.
- Article 2. Address of Agency.
- Article 3. Area of operation of Agency.
- Article 4. Aims & Objectives of Agency.
- Article 5. Membership
A. **Every Adult Female/Male can become a member of this agency subject to the condition that**
    1. She/ He should be mentally stable.
    2. Her/ His age is more than 18 years.
    3. She /He bear good moral character.
    4. Agrees with the aims & objectives & the constitution of the agency.
    5. Regularly pays membership fee.
    6. Permanently resides or operate business within area of operation of agency.
B. **Nature of Membership**
    1. **Ordinary Membership:** each person who pays Rs. 500/- annually for ordinary membership can become its members.
    2. **Life Membership:** each one who pays Rs. 10,000/- as lump sum membership fee can become its members.
    3. **Honorary Membership:** Person who can be helpful to the agency due to its knowledge, experience & deep interest in Social Welfare Activities or its affiliated with such agency which can be helpful for achieving the objectives of this agency can be nominated by the agency as honorary member of the agency. Condition of payment membership fee or being resident of its operational area will not be applicable to such membership.
    4. **Patron:** The agency may request a person whose services can be beneficial for progress & improvement of the Agency's Program, to become it's patron, subject to the condition that he pay Rs. 50,000/- as lump sum contribution to the agency & ready to accept it patron ship.

C. **Modus-Operandi for Seeking Membership:** Each person who is continuously eligible for membership & wishes to seek ordinary or life, shall apply for it on prescribed form to the Executive Body. Executive Body is empowered to accept or reject their applications. In case of rejection, the Executive Body will intimate in writing the reason of rejection application.

    1. **Honorary Member:** Under the article 5 (B) (3), The Executive Body may nominate any person as Honorary Member.

    2. **Patron:** Each one who under the article 5 (B) (4) fulfills conditions can become its patron.

D. **Modus-Operandi in case of rejection of application for membership:** Each one whose application has been rejected by The Executive Body may appeal to the General Body, the decision of which will be final.

E. **Rights of Members:**

    1. Ordinary or Life members will be member of its General Body. They have a right to vote & contest election.

    2. Honorary Member or Patron has no right to vote. They can participating in proceeding of meetings & express their opinion/ ideas.

F. **Suspension or Cancellation of Membership:** membership can be suspended / cancelled subject to:

    1. If a member don't pay membership fee immediately after its expiry, his membership shall stand suspended & if he fails to pay his membership fee within one month, his membership stand as cancelled.

    2. If with proper intimation one fails to attend 3 consecutive meetings of General Body or Executive Body without intimation & proper reason, General Body or Executive Body is empowered to cancel his membership.

    3. If the Executive Body has solid reasons that the conduct of the member is against the aims of the agency or is of defaming nature, The Executive Body will seek explanation. In case of unsatisfactory explanation The Executive Body will issue warning or shall demand resignation of his membership.

    4. If a member refuses to resign or don't mend his conduct, The Executive Body 3/4mejority can cancel his membership with reasons in writing

    5. If any member likes to resign voluntarily, The Executive Body is authorized to accept his resignation subject to the condition that he has paid all the dues.

G. **Restoration of Membership:**

    1. If a member whose membership has been suspended pays his dues, his membership automatically stands restores. A member, whose membership has been cancelled, has to apply a fresh for membership.

    2. Member whose membership has been cancelled has a right of appeal to the general body, the decision of which will be final.

- Article 6: Administrative Structure.

The agency consists of The General Body & Executive Body.

A. General Body
   1. Formation: The General Body shall consist of ordinary & life members.
   2. Power & Rights:
      - Formation of policy.
      - Shall elect the member of Executive Body.
      - Shall approve the proceedings of meetings.
      - Shall accord approval of Annual Report after due consideration.
      - Shall decide over vote of No confidence to final concurrence by the constitution.
      - Shall approve proposed amendments, but these amendments shall be subject to final concurrence by the constitution in other clauses.
      - Shall use all powers given in other articles of this constitution.

B. Formation of Executive Body.
   1. The Executive Body shall consist of ___07___ office bearers & ___04___ members who will be elected by the General Body.
   2. Duties & Rights
      - The Executive Body shall strive & take practical steps for achieving the aims & objects of agency in accordance with the policy guideline laid down by the General Body.
      - Shall be responsible for internal, administrative & financial matters & shall take necessary steps in this connection.
      - Shall fill in its vacant seat if it occurs in last half period of its functioning. If this occurs in first half period, then this seat shall be filled in through General Body.
      - Shall select a scheduled bank for its financial operation.
      - Shall prepare Annual Report & future budget, the concurrence of which shall be sought from the general body.
      - Shall use all powers given in other articles of this constitution.

- Office Bearers
  1. President
  2. Vice President- I
  3. Vice President- II
  4. General Secretary
  5. Joint Secretary
  6. Treasure/ finance Secretary
  7. Propaganda & Publication Secretary/ Press Secretary

(Rights & Powers)

1. President:

- She / he shall be the constitutional head of this agency & shall preside over all General / Executive Body Meetings.
- Is authorized to incur expenditure up to Rs, 25,000/- lump sum to achieve its objectives, the approval of which will be sought from the Executive Body in its next meeting.
- In situation of equal votes, she/he uses special opinion.
- Is authorized to postpone the proceedings of meeting being held in unruly.

2. Vice President- I
Shall use all powers of President in times of her/his absence.

3. Vice President- II
Shall use all powers of President in times of the absence of president & vice president I.

4. General Secretary
- Shall be general secretary of both the sides.
- Shall call meeting of Executive/ General Body with the consultation/ consent of president & shall issue agenda.
- Shall record the proceedings of regular meetings & seek concurrence from the president in its text meeting.
- Shall keep the record of the agency in his custody & shall be protector agency's property.
- Shall present annual report to the General Body after its approval from Executive Body.
- Is authorized from an expenditure upto Rs. 10,000/- lump sum, the approval of which shall be sought in next Executive Body meeting.

5. Joint Secretary
Shall use all powers & perform all duties of General Secretary in times of his absence & shall perform all perform all duties assigned to him by General Secretary.

6. Treasure/ Finance Secretary
- Shall be responsible for expenditure & other financial matters.
- Shall present monthly income/ expenditure statement to the Executive Body in its meeting.
- Shall get the accounts audited from the appointed chartered accountant & shall keep in custody the donation & membership copies & deposit all amounts received thereof in the bank.
- Is authorized to keep Rs. 5000/- as an earnest money for expenditure.

7. Propaganda & Publication Secretary/ Press Secretary
Shall be responsible for propaganda & publication.

8. Other authority of Office Barrier
In addition to the above mentioned authorities, all other powers rest with them as mentioned in other articles of this constitution.

- **Article 8. Conduct of Meetings**

Issuance of agenda to its member is compulsory for calling meetings of Executive/ General Body members.

If president or general secretary don't call meeting of Executive/ General Body for inspire of repeated requests of members, the members of general body shall issue "call meeting notice" of seven days to president or general secretary, even then, meeting is not called in themselves, then the concerned members are authorized to call meeting, shall issue agenda to its member through "Registered Cover". The decision of meeting shall be constitutionally valid.

- **Article 9. Duration of Notice & Quorum for General Body**
    - ✓ 15 days notice for election or regular meetings.
    - ✓ 7 days notice for special meetings.
    - ✓ 2 days notice for urgent meetings.

    Compulsory:

    Participants 1/3 of its total members is compulsory; otherwise the meeting shall stand postponed. Quorum is not compulsory for postponed meeting.

- **Article 10. Duration of Notice & Quorum of Executive Body**
    1. To call regular meeting 10 days notice, 3 days notice for special meeting & 24 hours for urgent meeting is necessary.
    2. The participation of 2/3 of its total members is compulsory for each meeting of executive body, otherwise the meeting shall stand postponed at next date for which condition of quorum is not compulsory.

- **Article 11. Finances**
    1. The Financial year of the agency shall be in accordance with the financial year of government of Pakistan.
    2. The signature of President or General Secretary shall be compulsory along with signature of Treasure for drawing from bank in times of absence of treasure, president & general secretary shall be authorized to sign the cheques.
    3. The income of the agency shall be utilized to achieve its set objectives.
    4. The annual audit of accounts of the agency shall be conducted by the chartered accountant or approved Auditor/ Auditors by the registration authority.

- **Article 12. Constitutional Amendment**
  The General Body shall call special meeting for amendment in the constitution & shall decide the proposed amendment by ¾ majority. The amendment shall be subject to final concurrence by the registration authority & shall not be operative prior to its concurrence.

- **Article 13. No Confidence Motion**

On the written demand of at least 1/3 of total members of executive body or general body no confidence motion against any office bearer can be moved in only general body meeting, the approval of which is subject to the approval of president members.

- **Article 14. Miscellaneous/ others**
    1. The duration of working of office bearers & members of executive body through election shall be for___03___years.
    2. Decisions on all matters (keeping aside such matters as specially mentioned in the constitution shall be taken on simple majority.)
    3. Counting of the vote in executive & general body meetings shall be through show of hand & if considered essential through "Secret Ballot"
- **Article 15. Voluntary Dissolution**
    If the members of the agency wish to voluntarily dissolve the agency, they shall have to act in accordance with section 11-12 of voluntary social welfare agencies (registration & control) ordinance, 1961.

Field of Services

1- Child Welfare
2- Youth Welfare
3- Women Welfare
4- Human Welfare
5- Disability, Family Planning
6- Recreational Services
7- Civil Education
8- Welfare of Prisoners
9- Welfare of Juvenile Delinquent
10- Welfare of Baggers, Widows & Needy
11- Patient Welfare
12- Welfare of Old & Infirm Persons
13- Training of Social Services
14- Coordination Among Social Welfare Institution
15- Welfare of Neglected Persons
16- Disaster Management

Types of NGOs & Legislation:

No.	Types of NGOs	Registered Process
1.	Societies	Registration Act, 1860
2.	Voluntary Social Welfare Agencies	Registration & Control Ordinance, 1961
3.	Cooperative Societies	Cooperative Societies Act, 1925
4.	Non – Profit Companies	Companies Ordinance, 1984

| 5. | Public Charitable Trust | Trust Act, 1882 |
| 6. | Charitable & Endowment Trust | Charitable Endowment Act, 1890 |

1. What is Societies Registration Act 1860?

"An Act for the Registration of Literary,
Scientific and Charitable Societies"

According to Societies Registration Act, 1860 the society may be registered for the grant of charitable assistance, for the promotion of science, literature, the fine arts, for instruction, the diffusion of useful knowledge, diffusion of political education the foundation or maintenance of libraries or reading rooms, public museums and galleries of paintings and other works of art, collection of natural history, mechanical and philosophical inventions, instruments or designs.

This Act applies to charitable societies with a wide range of public benefit purposes.

Societies Registration Act, 1860

1- Societies formed by memorandum of association and registration. Any 7 or more persons associated for any literary, scientific or charitable purpose, or for any such purpose which is described by society.
2- Memorandum of association shall contain the following things.
   - ❖ Name of Society
   - ❖ Objectives of Society
   - ❖ Address
   - ❖ A copy of Rules & Regulations of Society
3- Registration fee shall be paid to the provisional government.
4- According to the rules of the society, the annual general meeting of the society is held once in every year.
5- The property which is belonged to a society registered under this Act, if not vested in trustees, shall be deemed to be vested, for the time being, in the governing body of such society, and in all proceedings, civil and criminal, may be described as the property of the governing body of such society by their proper title.
6- Every society registered under this Act may sue or be sued in the name of the president, chairman, or principal secretary, or trustees, as shall be determined by the rules and regulations of the society, and, in default of such determination, in the name of such person as shall be appointed by the governing body for the occasion:

Provided that it shall be competent for any person having a claim or demand against the society, to sue the president or chairman, or principal secretary or the trustees thereof, if on application to the governing body some other officer or person be not nominated to be the defendant.

7- Suits are not to abate.
8- If a judgment shall be recovered against the person or officer named on behalf of the society, such judgment shall not be put in force against the property, or against the body of such person or officer, but against the property of the society.
9- Recovery of penalty accruing under bye-law.
10- Members liable to be sued as strangers – Recovery by successful defendant of costs adjudged.
11- The guilty of the members of offences punishable as strangers.
12- Societies enabled to alter, extend or abridge their purposes.

13- Provision for dissolution of societies and adjustment of their affairs of the Assent required & government consent.
14- Upon a dissolution no member to receive profit & Clause not to apply to joint-stock companies.
15- Member defined that why disqualified members.
16- Governing Body has defined the rules & regulations to all its members.
17- Registration of societies formed before Act – Assent required.
18- Such societies to file memorandum, etc., with Registrar of Joint-Stock Companies.
19- Inspection of documents – Certified Copies.
20- To what societies Act or works for appling.
21- Registration of Deeni Madaris.

2. What are the Voluntary Social Welfare Agencies (Registration & Control Ordinance, 1961)?
Those agencies who works for the welfare of society as a voluntary.

1- Short title, extent and commencement.
This Ordinance may be called the Voluntary Social Welfare Agencies (Registration and Control) Ordinance, 1961.
- It extends to the whole of the Punjab
- It shall come into force on such date as the government may, by notification in the official Gazette, appoint in this behalf.
2- Definitions: "voluntary social welfare agency" means an organization, association or undertaking established by persons of their own free will for the purpose of rendering welfare services in any one or more of the fields mentioned in the Schedule and depending for its resources on public subscriptions, donations or Government aid.
3- Prohibition against establishing or continuing an agency without registration.
4- Application for registration, etc.
5- Establishment and continuance agency.
6- Appeal.
7- Conditions to be complied with by registered agencies.

8- Amendment of the constitution of registered agency.
9- Suspension or dissolution of governing bodies of registered agencies.
10- Dissolution of registered agency.
11- Voluntary dissolution of registered agency.
12- Consequences of dissolution.
13- Inspection of documents, etc.
14- Penalties and procedure.
15- Indemnity.
16- Power to amend schedule.
17- Power to exempt.
18- Delegation of powers.
19- Rules.

3. What are the Cooperative Societies & Cooperative Societies Act, 1925?

It is a sometime of farm, business, or other organization which is owned and run jointly by its members, who share the profits or benefits. In Multan, it is working on the projects of societies such as Wapda town etc.

To facilitate the formation and working of Co-operative Societies for the promotion of thrift, self-help and mutual aid among agriculturists and other persons with common economic needs so as to bring about better living, better business; the act Cooperative Societies, 1925 was promulgated for the Provinces of Pakistan.

There are some acts of Cooperative Society of 1925 which are as followed.
1- This Act may be called the Cooperative Societies Act, 1925.
2- This Act extends to the [Punjab/Singh/N.W.F.P./Baluchistan] whole of the Province except the Tribal Area.
3- **Definitions.** In this Act, unless there is anything repugnant in the subject or context!
- **"bye-laws"** means bye-laws registered under this Act and for the time being in force and includes a registered amendment of such bye-laws;
- **"Committee"** means the Committee of Management or other directing body to whom the management of the affairs of a society is entrusted;
- **"Financing Bank"** Means a society the main object of which is to make loans in cash or in kind to any other society or to any agriculturist who is not a member of a society or to both societies and such agriculturists;
- **"Member"** includes a person joining in the application for the registration of a society or a person admitted to membership after registration in accordance with the rules and bye-laws applicable to such society;
- **"Officer"** includes a chairman, secretary, treasurer, member of committee or other person empowered under the rules or under the bye laws of a society to give directions in regard to the business of such society;
- **"Society"** means a society registered or deemed to be registered under this Act;

- **"Registrar"** means a person appointed to perform the duties of a Registrar of Cooperative Societies under this Act;
- **"Rules"** means rules made under this act;
- Resource society
  - ➤ Producer society
  - ➤ Consumer society
  - ➤ Housing society
  - ➤ General society

4- The Provincial Government may appoint a person to be Registrar of Cooperative Societies for the Province or any portion of it, and may appoint a person or persons to assist such Registrar, and may, by general or special order, confer on any such person or persons all or any of the powers of a Registrar under this Act.
- Power of Registrar to issue search warrant.

5- Societies which may be registered.

6- Restrictions on interest of member of society with limited liability and a share capital.

7- Power of Registrar to decide certain questions

8- Application for registration

9- Registration.

10- Evidence of Registration.

11- Annual General Meeting

12- Special General Meeting

13- Amalgamation & transform of society

14- Amendment of the bye-laws of a society

15- No rights of membership to be exercised till due payments are made

16- One of the members of society to vote in the affair of this society.

17- Restrictions on transfer of share or interest

18- Address of societies.

19- Copy of Act, etc. to be open to inspection

20- Audit

21- Societies to be bodies corporate.

22- Prior claim of society

23- Charge and set-off in respect of shares or interest of member

24- Share or interest not liable to attachment

25- Register of members

26- Admissibility of copy of entry as evidence.

27- Exemption form compulsory registration of instruments relating to shares of society

28- Power to exempt form income Tax duty, registration and court fees

29- Restrictions on loans.

30- Restrictions on borrowing

31- Restrictions on other transactions with non-members

32- Investment of funds

33- Restrictions on dividend

34- Reserve funds

35- Restrictions on distribution of profit

36- Provident funds

37- Contribution to charitable purpose

38- Inquiry by registrar
39- Inspection of books of indebted society
- Inspection of books by financing bank
40- Power of Registrar to exercise powers under Section 50-A in the course of an inquiry or inspection.
41- Power to remove officers.
42- Power of Registrar to give directions.
43- Special measures
44- Cost of inquiry
45- Recovery of cost
46- Society may be wound up if membership is reduced.
47- Effect of cancellation of registration
48- Power of Registrar to assess damage against delinquent promoters
49- Bar of suit in winding up and dissolution matters
50- Disposal of surplus assets
51- Surplus assets of housing society
52- Everyone who do any crime get the punishment as a stranger
53- Rules & regulations

4. What are the Non Profit Companies & Companies Ordinance 1984?

Non Profit Company is a type of company or organization that does not earn profits for its owners. All of the money which is earned, donated to a nonprofit organization and it is used for the welfare of people & also it is included in the organization's objectives. Typically non-profit companies or organizations are charities or other types of public service organizations.

Companies Ordinance 1984

Associations not for profit are formed under section 42 of the Companies Ordinance, 1984, according to the ordinance there are 2 types of associations established for non-profit basis. An Association not for profit is an organization formed for the purpose of serving public or for mutual benefit other than pursuit of benefits. According to Section 42 of the Companies Ordinance, 1984 the main objects of the Association are for promoting commerce, art, science, religion, sports, social services, charity or any other useful object, and applies or intends to apply its profits, if any, or other income in promoting its objects. The Association shall on registration enjoy all the privileges of a limited company and be subject to all its obligations, except those of using the words Limited, Private Limited or Guarantee Limited. To get registered an Association for non-profit purposes first is to obtain license under Section 42 of the Ordinance from Securities & Exchange Commission of Pakistan and thereafter to register the Association as a company. The association is generally a guarantee limited company having no share capital.

5. What is the Public Charitable Trust, Trust Act 1882?

A charitable trust is specifically set up to hold and protect assets for charitable purposes. It can be set up to aid in the relief of poverty, the advancement of education or religion, or any other matter for public benefit.

Trust Act, 1882

A trust is established under the Trusts Act, 1882. For this type of trust, the three conditions of a creator, trustee and beneficiary being present, are unconditional requirements. A public charitable trust is a trust which is established for the benefit of the society or at least a certain section of society. There are no particular laws relating to public trusts. However, the rules in the Trust Act of 1882 can be applied to the public and charitable trusts. In the case of public charitable trusts, the conditions governing private trusts are equally important. However, if the objectives are not clear, unlike the private trusts, these trusts would be sustained as long as there is an intention of charity.

- There must be some trust property, whether in cash or capital assets (land or buildings)
- The objectives of the trust must be charitable or for the benefit of society

The application for the registration of trust requires the following:

- Particulars of documents creating the trust.
- Particulars of the trustees and the beneficiaries.
- Details of what the trust property is going to be. There is no minimum value of property for starting a trust. If the property is an immovable property then the transfer deed shall be on a stamp paper on the value of the property and it shall be registered.
- Preparation of the trust deed, that is, i.e. declaration of having created a public charitable trust.

6) What is the Charitable & Endowment Trust & Charitable & Endowment Act 1890?

An act to provide for the vesting & administration of property held in trust for charitable purpose. There are some acts of this trust which are as followed.

1. Title, extend and commencement: this act is also called the Charitable & endowment Act 1890.
2. In this Act "Charitable purpose" includes relief of the poor, education, medical relief and the advancement of any other object of general public utility, but does not include a purpose which relates exclusively to religious teaching or worship.
3. Appointments and Incorporation of Treasurer of Charitable Endowments
4. Appropriate Government
5. Orders 'vesting property in Treasurer
6. Schemes for administration of property vested in the Treasurer
7. Mode of applying for vesting orders and schemes
8. Exercise by Governor-General-in-Council of powers of Local Government
9. Bare trusteeship of Treasurer
10. Annual publication of list of properties vested in Treasure
11. Provisions for continuance of office of Treasurer in certain contingencies
12. Transfer of property from one Treasurer to another
13. Rules & Regulations
14. Indemnity to Government and Treasurer
15. Saving with respect to Advocate-General and Official Trustee

SOS Children Village

Introduction

SOS is stand for "SAVE OUR SOULS". SOS Children Village is a Private Social Welfare Organization. It is providing orphans & abandoned children a home, good nurturing & a fair chance in life. A new & permanent home. The children remain in SOS Care until they are able to lead independent lives.

What we want for the World Children?

- Every Child belongs to a family.
- Every Child Grows with love.
- Every Child Grows with respect.
- Every Child Grows with security.

Affiliation SOS Children's Village of All Pakistan

Types of Facility	Number	Beneficiaries
SOS Children's Villages	473	56971
SOS Youth Facilities	383	15552
SOS Kindergartens	226	22200
SOS Hermanno Gmeiner High Schools	185	103832
SOS Vocational Training Centers	61	13526
SOS Social Centers	499	420482
SOS Medical Centers	60	452543
SOS Emergencies Relief Programs	10	61528
Total	1897	1146640

Present Services & Beneficiaries of Multan

Serial No.	Name of Services	No. of Units	No. of Beneficiaries
1.	SOS Children Village	1	140 (orphans & abandoned children)
2.	SOS Hermanno Gmeiner High School Multan	1	600 (Students)

4 Basic Principles

The philosophy of SOS is very simple & basic that Every Child has the right to good nurturing. In order to achieve this 4 principles are adhered to & form the basis of all the work of the organization.

1- A Mother
2- Brothers & Sisters
3- A home
4- A village

SOS Village Multan

The SOS Children Village Multan is one of the more recent projects to be established & was opened in the summer of 2002. The land for this project, as well as for the school, has been donated by the government of the Punjab. The village has 17 family homes along with other requirement such as auditorium, mosque, grocery, shop, workshops, administrative office, essential staff residence etc. The architectural design is exceptionally attractive & features traditional brick work combined with local elements. Before the new premises was ready a temporary children's homes began in 1999, so 70 every excited children were ready to move into their new homes. This is the first welfare project of its kind in Multan & has been very well received by the community.

 ➢ SOS Children Village is being run by the well reputed, credible & GOD fearing volunteers. The organization is working up to the standard/ criteria set by the social welfare, women development & Bait-ul-mal departments.

SOS Hermanno Gmeiner High School Multan

SOS Hermanno Gmeiner High School Multan is a non-profit educational institution, only dedicated to promote quality education in remote & much neglected areas of Multan. The first SOS Hermanno GmeinerSchool was opened in 1989 in Lahore. All construction work done through donations for local & multinational corporate groups & individuals, but land been provided by the government of Pakistan. Since then SOS has established another 5 schools in Karachi, Rawalpindi, Fasailabad, Sialkot & Sargodha. SOS Hermanno Gmeiner High School Multan is the most recent establishment of SOS Pakistan. But now it has been working for the children of SOS village & few children for the community.

SOS Multan had identified Muza Hamid Pur, Muza Ali Pur as its target areas for the SOS Hermanno Gmeiner High School. The area was selected based on the need to provide quality education for the children of both Hamid Pur & Ali Pur. The most prominent problem the area is the invariability of high school for especially for girls. People usually lead lives below the poverty lines. Main source of income is temporary labor work in any nearby- mill or factory.

SOS Hermanno Gmeiner High School Multan is a project of SOS children Village Multan. It is affiliated with the SOS Children Villages of Pakistan & SOS Kinderdorf International. SOS Hermanno Gmeiner High School is working all over the world since 1950, with over 200 projects in more than 100 countries. The SOS Hermanno Gmeiner High School is not only providing premier education to the orphans & abandoned children of SOS Children Villages but it also insuring the high standard of education for the neglected of remote communities. The school runs on a non income generation basis with a minimum fee charge of Rs. 250/- per month. Syllabus books & note books are provided to the children free or charge. The school encourages children from low income areas to receive standard education regardless of their financial limitations. The school also offers free scholarships to those children, who may unable to pay even the nominal fee charged by the school.

The school offers classes from play group till Matric, following an English Medium base of education, to equip the neglected children to face the competitive world of today with the weapon of education in their hand. SOS Hermanno Gmeiner High School Multan adopted a very modern education system & children will receive education through computers & audio video methodology of teaching.

Yearly Activities

The Multan Village has seen much activity throughout the year. Various Schools & collages & institution have been visiting periodically & interacting with our children. Large well known corporate organizations such as Telenor Pakistan, Coca Cola Bverages Pvt. Ltd, Shell

Pakistan, Novartis & KFC organized interesting events with our children both at the village & at external locations. We have also organizing seminars, awareness campaign & different events like Basant Mela, Musical Evenings, Cricket Tournaments, Fun fair, Sports Week & Celebrating International Days throughout the years. SOS Children Village Multan celebrated its 10th anniversary on 28th February 2009. Principal Officer of American General Consulate of Pakistan Mr. Barian D. Hunt specially visited SOS Multan Projects along with Public Affairs, Officers US Consulate Ms. Treesi Meal & cultural affairs officers US Consulate Tahira Habib.

Future Program

A high school will be established at the industrial state sector one where about 1000 students may get education.

Financial Position of NGO

The NGO has sound financial position to run the welfare activity at their own level.

Shaoor Development Organization

Name: Shaoor Development Organiation

Address: 317 Sher Shah Road Jalilabad Colony Multan

Date of Establishment: 28-1-2002

Number & Date of Registration: DOSW (MN)/ 352 dated 7-1-2003

Registration Act: Registration & Control Ordinance 1961

Aims & Objectives:
- Child Welfare: establishment of the formal & informal educational institutions.
- Youth Welfare
  - ✓ Sports
  - ✓ To take the steps for stopping Narcotics drugs.
  - ✓ To help the youth for getting the employment
- Women Welfare
  - ✓ To establish industrial home
  - ✓ To provide the technical, legal & economical help to defenseless women
- Patient Welfare
  - ✓ To provide help in proper treatment
  - ✓ To establishment of free dispensaries
  - ✓ Mobile Camp
- General Public Welfare
  - ✓ To create the cooperation or understanding between the Social Welfare institutions or department.
  - ✓ To create the technical affiliation between the institutions of Social Welfare.
  - ✓ Save the environment & Sanitation Program
  - ✓ Tree plantation

Financial Resources: Local Great/ Donation

Audit Report:

Receipt
Cash: 1 July 2010

Donations & Subscription

Grant from HG & M	160000
Subciption Membership fees	90000
Donation (Cash)	600500
Contribution	456000
Income From Agencies own services (Specify) kills centre fee	25000
Consultancy & services	45500
	1493900

Receipts & payments account for the year ended

Payments	Rupees
Administrative Expenses	
Salaries & Allowances	120400
Travelling & Convaince	70000
Training Local	50200
Training National	80200
Utility Expenditure	60500
Communication Expenditure	90000
Printing & Stationarry	120000
Miscellaneous	25500
	616800

Program Expenses

Capacity Building	70500
Environment Campaign	145000
Youth Development	70000
Health Care Education	120000
Women Development	145000
Literacy Program	65000
Advocacy Compaign	110500
	726000

Cash 30 June 2011 → 151100
Cash & Bank Balance
Total Rupees → 1493900

President   General Secretary   Treasure

Auditors' Report
    We have checked the above receipts & payments account of "Shaoor Development Organization" Sher Shah Road Multan for the year ended the account in agreement with the books of account provide to us.

Place: Multan
Dated: 20-7-2011
Raja & Company

Women Festival 2003
    The basic points of women festival of 2003
    • Supervision Sport & Cultural Committee District Multan
    • Shaoor Development Voluntary Social Welfare Agencies

- Awareness provide community about female rights & also show income generating protects for women
- Voluntary Social Welfare Agencies show the works of industrial home of females
  - ✓ Clothes
  - ✓ Painting works
  - ✓ Cooking items
  - ✓ For students literature & consultancy of social welfare projects
- Blind centers
- Education department for women development
- Embroidery
- Family planning
- Forest department → social Development

  - ■ Literature & News
  - ■ Human Awareness
  - ■ Growing Plantation
- Fouji Foundation → Courses for females
- Public Health nursing school Nishter Hospital Multan
- Awareness for fundamental basic rights for female.
- The main theme was that women are the important part of society but they ignored. Women rights ignorance also becomes the reason of ignorance of representative seats in district, government, provisional & national assembly.
- Work for women empowerment.

Other works or seminar of this organization
- Children Conference 23-25 December 2006
- Jashn-e-baharan & Republic Day of Pakistan
  - ✓ 22 March 2007
  - ✓ Fair for children & women
  - ✓ Arranged → CACL Punjab(Collation Against Child Labor)
  - ✓ Held → Population Department Multan & MC Middle School Kari Daood Khan Multan
- Workshop & training about to save the environment
  - ✓ Walk for saving the environment
  - ✓ 4-5 june 2007
- Women development seminar distribution certificate & prizes 10-9-2007 (women vocational training center project no. 11)
- Ceremony distribution the school uniform 20-9-2007 (Women Jail Multan for course for residence children with CACL Spark NGO)
- Candle light evening on the child day 14-20 November 2007
- South Punjab Children Conference 15 Nov 2007 with CACL Punjab Spark
- Seminar about Growing Plantation 29 May 2009 Friday 10 Am. (Resource Center for Women Councilors (Grap) near Girls Hostel Sanatzar)

- 2nd Seminar about Growing Plantation 5 June 2009 10 Am. (Dawoo Bus Service Workshop Khanewal Multan)
- Seminar & Dangi 14 Feb 2012 place: Function Hall Oxford High School Multan
- Seminar about Anti Narcotics Drugs Nijat Center Multan 20-26 June 2012
- Awareness Compaign Dangi 12 May 2012 (promotion of awareness & environmental control of dangi) Place: Memorial Youth Club
- Seminar at dengi 31 Aug 2012. Place: Govt. Nusrat-ul-Islam High Secondary School Multan Cant
- International Day to Save environment 4-5-6 June 2013 Deparment of Save the Environment Multan & Department of Social Welfare & Bait-ul-mal
- Ceremony at get rid of child labor Multan 10-11-12 June 2013
  - 10 June 2013 in Hotel Shelton one "Finishing for domestic child labor media forum"
  - 11 June 2013 "Finishing for domestic child labor conference office CRC Mulatn"
  - 12 June 2013 "Demonstration on stopping Child Labor Press Club Multan"
- Ceremony at Anti Narcotics Drugs. Place: Anti Narcotics force Punjab.

Society for Special Persons

Name: Society for Special Persons

Address: Chanab Club near Bag Langay Khan Multan

President: Zahida Hameed 0321-6315160

Registration Act: Registration & Control Ordinance 1961

Aims & Objectives:
- To work for disabled people especially handicapped
- For better life of handicapped people to make the better Education system
- To make the understanding or coordination between social organizations
- To provide training of social serving

Field/Area of Service: Provisions of wheel chairs to the special persons

Future Program:
- Data collection of working organization
- Data collection for need assessment for special persons & planning on the basis of data collection.

Other works or seminar of this organization
- Report on meeting with Edo financing & planning regarding accessibility of persons with disabilities.
- Wheel chair distribution ceremony District Rajan Pur 7 June 2013
- Inauguration Ceremony of wheel Chair accessible Ranp in PIA office Multan
- National Political Conference 22 Oct 2012
- First accessibility day 22 Oct 2011 (first world accessibility day "Access to All")
- Media Response

Sawail Development Organization

Name: Swail Development Organization

Address: Kutcheri Road Multan

Chairperson : Yasmeen Khakwani

Registration Act: Registration & Control Ordinance 1961

Focus: Women & Children

Aims & Objectives:
- Child welfare (to work for child labor & child welfare)
- Women welfare (training skills centers will be established for women)
- Family planning
- Social Services Training
- Youth welfare (to work for the unemployed youth & try to make them employed)
- Recreational program & activities will be held

Administration Staff:
1. President
2. Vice President
3. Vice President 2
4. General Secretary
5. Joint Secretary
6. Finance Secretary
7. Press Secretary/ Secretary information & technology

Other works or seminar of this organization
- Seminar on women violence day at Multan Law Collage 26 Nov 2013
- Seminar on special children at Multan Law collage 3 Dec 2013
- World Health Day at CHC Hospital 6 April 2013
- International Thalasemia Day 22 May 2013
- Pakistan Women Day 13 Feb 2013
- Seminar on drug rehabilitation day 25 June 2008
- Seminar about role of civil defense & civil society in condition of rescue of 1122. 28 June 2010
- Work of SPARC at CRC (Child Rights Committee) & CACL (Collation Against Child Labor)
- Seminar about Human, Women & Child Rights according to on Charter 5 March 2011 Bosan Town Hall Multan.

Citizens Community Board (CCB)

- In CCB, the committee is made of 7 union councils. One person is chairman. 25 members are necessary in them.
- Firstly they are registered.
- Multan have total 6 towns → 4 cities, 1 Jalalpur, 1 shujaabad
- This project can be done at 3 levels; union council, town & district level. You can apply for any field.
- Project starting costs

  ✓ Union Council → 1 lack
  ✓ Town → 30/40 lack
  ✓ District → 75 lack
- After submitting projects, CCB submit the 20% & government pay 80%. Government provides this pay in 3 episodes.
- Meeting report is based on nazim of area, chairman of CCB & planning of DO.
- After this which report is prepared, this report is send to Community development office for signature after this it send to finance Edo for checking that how they use the government payment.
- According to Punjab government, no any project is not more than of 7.5 million.
- This project is only for the local communities not of personal benefit or for commercial use.

Criticism and Suggestion

During observation of social welfare departments and NGOs I feel that

- All Social Welfare Departments & NGOs always conduct the seminars & awareness programs in front those people who already know about the social evil of society & always invited the officers, school, collage & university teachers & many other employees who already know about them. We have to need to aware the common people not of officers.

- We always talk about many social evils but not act upon them. For example, we attend the seminar about finishing discrimination but in our houses we don't act upon them because we are just man of words, not of deed. Just for seeing, we take the example of women international day. 8th March, we celebrate International Women Day. What do you think can this day give the equal rights to women, all bad customs will be finished towards females? No, because we are just man of words, we are just GOD of words, not of deeds.

➤ I am not in favor of NGOs that have we not as like power that we finish these social evils of our society from our own hands? For finishing the bad evils , we have to take the help of others countries. According to my point of view, No, we should not take the help from other countries because we give our weak points to other countries through the work of NGOs. We have to need to make strong. Government laws should strictly refer to public who don't act upon them, give them very hard punishment. Everyone do their own welfare who are weak just teach them right way for solving their problem that said them they will solve their problem now to their own self. We have to adopt the system of China that don't give the fish for eating, teach them the method of catching the fish & cooking it & after this said him that now you do your work & now this person is on the way of progress that he caught the fish & cook it for his own self. As like One day, we have no need of any NGO & we will be at the way of progress and it is the right way of the welfare of our people, community, society and also our country because we should never forget that GOD always help those who help themselves then here is no need of NGOs & Social Welfare Departments.